The Silences of Fire

The Silences of Fire

Tom Marshall

London
Macmillan & Co. Ltd.
1969

Printed in Canada for The Macmillan Company of Canada Ltd. 70 Bond Street, Toronto 2

Acknowledgements

Acknowledgements are due to the following: *Alphabet, The Beast With Three Backs* (Quarry Press), *The Cambridge Review, The Canadian Forum, Delta, Edge, The Fiddlehead,* The Hudson's Bay Company, *The Literary Review, The New Romans* (M. G. Hurtig), *New Voices of the Commonwealth* (Evans), *The Penguin Book of Canadian Verse, Poetry One 1968* (London), *Quarry, The Queen's Quarterly, The Southern Review* (Adelaide), *Talon, The Tamarack Review, Tribune* (London), and *Yes.*

Contents

These Islands

Macdonald Park

Dedication: 5 Lines For Love

when the clean snow
falls into sunlight
for the merest instant

I know your body
lives in the world

The Burning Man

The park is more like a wood

Dream

The park is more like a wood.
The great trees stand apart
at a respectful distance.

On the night we walk
into the park, lightning falls
and fails, a sensuality turned inward.

Overhead, in waves, the lost fringes
of forest blow, break
under the ghostly stars, and the

early moon bends, beckoning
our lips and bodies back. At this point,
always, I turn and speak to you.

From Here

Beyond the park is the lake.
I cannot see it
from my balcony.

But I see today
a child in the park
running the hard ground
under the red sky, and I

am taken suddenly back
to the favourite photograph,
memory of a memory,
me, leaning, grinning round

1

the corner of the great tree
laughing the invisible lake,

and I can take that child
as a dwarf of me,
even from here I can see
all the elements are there
heart can find, mind can be —
fire, earth, water, air,
the child in the wood
who laughed around the tree.

Summer

Sun blooms in our bodies
like a soft death,
a warmth that is far
more permanent than love.

We imagine that sun
becomes part of us.
Fools not to know
we must fall into it.

For now the park
opens within, living trees
unlock their secrets
to the whole silence of fire.

And do not ask to love me
but love through me
as now through the ripe tree
the bruise of life burns outward.

Fall

Not only children inherit the park
now the park is a yellow stillness
but old men, perverts of several kinds,
grotesque women with floppy hats and sunglasses –
sitting on benches among their squirrels,
day after day feeding on leaves and paper.

Alone, I watch them from my balcony
as from a dark doorway. I know
they have gone under the hanging leaves
to give themselves to the park.
They would like to sink into the earth
to nourish a tree.

I watch. And I think I see.
Into delicious depths of self-abasement
they are falling. Offering at last
to the unmoved autumnal corridors
the bitter love of the unbeautiful.
So that the world opens, flows.
The park grows wider than light.

For those
who court the earth court not obscenity
but use. O love's too pitiful a word
to comprehend the kindness of the place
that offers them such death –
death eternal, the passion of the earth
trembling at the root of their design.

3

Day by day they come. And I watch
from the balcony.

                    (O see
beyond the trees that tower up to heaven
the burning man fall outward into ardent space)

Niagara

You the beginning
of all
my stormy journey
closer
and closer to terror.

For truth is also terror.
In the riding wind
stand
like disintegrating oracles
the widening rounds
of your roses.

To survive
I would want
to see you
with the cold
detachment of a god.

I know
it is
because of you
intolerant of weakness
I go

my heart-sick
bold
broken-tongued way
to wisdom
and the doubtful rectitude
of controllable despair.

Autobiographies

I

I ate the mint-leaves among the railway cinders.
The sun flamed, at night the trains rumbled, the water-
fall roared: the town splayed upon the terrible fountain.
On the air floats Ponce de Leon's gaudy illusion:
the fast cars, the fast girls who opened their legs,
drunk over the river, roaring in Buffalo,
stumbling over beer-cans on the midnight beaches.
In dreams I slid into the crashing waters
so easily, so easily I thought all waters
lived in my veins and flowed in living fountains.
The blackshirt hoods lounged sulkily on Centre St.,
dark guardians of human pain, warning angels
with truths too simple for the roaring boys.
The mirror of Narcissus lay hid in the wood
a dark enamelled pool flecked with angry stars.

II

The groundhogs nuzzling at the window-panes
in the brilliant moonlight have awakened me
from superb dreams of holocaust and retribution.
These brilliant, restless nights, the torments of hay-fever
exacerbate the itch in the shocked brain.
A woman sleeps, or does not sleep, in another room.
Her white hair electric, outspread, fills the moonlit
    windows,
she lies against the night and the angry stars
of ten, perhaps twenty years. An owl's cry
is all but lost in the reckless barrage of moonlight,
the loud torrent that breaks and conquers the grotesque
    shapes
of groundhogs, trees, badgers or whatever wakes.
The wood is lunatic, shaken with incandescent life.
In this house of illness, guilt and moonlight
I am pierced by the white, corrosive eye of God.

The Mother in Wartime. The Child After.

I

It was a kind
of secret sainthood.
Tending her Hiroshima flowers.
We travelled in south country
coming to rest nowhere.

In the Joplin, Mo.,
backyard, the barren fig-tree.
The blacks lurched, sang
in the cramped back-lanes.
Jimmy called them "boogie-men".

Somewhere, tanks and guns were firing.
Trees in the middle distances
with strange birds.
In house, the man and the woman
move in a vast silence.

II

North, silence, and green.
Strange flowers float on the blood.
Hollyhock, lilac-tree
taller than children.
Fever burns north away.

See, now the skies flower.
Annunciation surely dogs us.
Flying saucers flash
like napalm.
In dreams the face burns:

A woman smitten by fire
cries: "I have seen a thing.
The godhead is a great wound
burning in the universe.
Like flowers burning in rain."

American Apocalypse: Collage with Headlines

*"Because to love is frightening we prefer
the freedom of our crimes."*
            – *Frank Templeton Prince,* "Soldiers Bathing"

To the south the violent Utopians rage
at this day.   SNIPER KILLS NAZI
Hell's Angels plant the flower girls.
Ahab wants to bomb his leviathan.

HIPPY'S GIRL RAPED BY FIVE NEGROES
At this day.   (Can there be a new man?
Can there be a fire that does not consume?
Ahab turn the ship home?)

The whale thrashes in the captain's guts.
(A man alone is terrified by love.)
Love's body is a map of burning flesh.
And poetry is newsprint, not pain.

UFO SIGHTED   STRANGLER THOUGHT INSANE
Love bombs his cities of dark flesh again.

10

Achilles Overcome

it is true the terrible death of the King
occurred   but in the fabled world
in the unbroken fabric of dream
where no belief is real

the Queen herself drowsy   and stumbling
in a daze of dark beauty   the King
slumped under the anguished hands
of myrmidons   the rose of his blood

opening beyond the sun's fragile zenith
the white haze of noon
the snakelike thrashing of crowd and motorcade

to silence   the silence of dead space
in slow convulsions of rose
from the black stem of a rifle-sight

Elegy

The astronaut is wed to space
The astronaut walks in the silences of fire

Introduction to "Don Quixote"

Until the fires of the last morning
Awaken out of burnished oak walls
That bound the monkish habits of our souls
Some bleak splendour, let us contemplate
The Absolute Absurdity, a Second Coming:
Refraction of the Word our comedy.

Note: For A.D. read Divine Anachronism.

In this romance, our latter-century Passion,
An errant knight cannot discern his dragon,
A scholar-saint, the new angelic doctor,
Proves beyond all reasonable doubt
That mysticism is ridiculous,
A comic Christ stretched on a giddy windmill
Succumbs again to the Judas kiss of a world's laughter.

Excalibur: The Returned Deserter

for Douglas LePan

After three martinis
one can be profound
and grateful too.

Gratitude comes hard
I admit.   By nature
I am more inclined
to criticize
unreasonably what cannot be helped.

You say that you came late
to what I know.
All of us come *too* late, of course,

but you
came at first with a cadenced grace
beyond the ordinary, a word
heraldic and ideal.   You come

now with earth
staining your healing blade
into something rich and rude,

breaking the pride
of angels to a shivering life,
passion and plenitude.

Lawrence

In Eastwood the miners are singing in the streets.
In Eastwood the miners in the roads are singing.
You look now with unspeakable longing at a gentian
knowing you must go down after all.

The blue coal-dust has settled inside you.
England's dust heavy with death and misery.
You saw England then as a sinking coffin.
In Eastwood the miners in the roads are singing.

Your mother will not have you go down.
But you come to the great sea, the centre of earth.
You seek the doorway to the Lords of Life.
In Eastwood the miners are singing in the streets.

Your father's face is blue with coal-dust.
He seeks to draw you down after him.
You flee him and you seek him everywhere.
In Eastwood the miners in the roads are singing.

Your mother was dragged down like Persephone.
She seeks to draw you down after her.
In Eastwood the miners are singing in the streets.
You sing your song, a blue flame, to Quetzalcoatl.

A serpent comes from the earth to the trough.
Lonely and golden, flesh of the sun's flesh.
You touch the side of a woman, lonely and golden.
She is triumphantly other, she is not you.

When the sun bursts the poppies are blood.
The gentians become unspeakably blue.
The red rivers reach to the pulsing sun.
In Eastwood the miners in the roads are singing.

15

In Eastwood the miners are singing in the streets.
You look now with unspeakable longing at a gentian
knowing you must go down at last.
This is another passage, you will come through.

Surely there was no more violence

Surely there was no more violence
in Hitler than in Van Gogh.
Today a woman told me
about wartime London.
On Friday the men sent a bus.
On Saturday the N.C.O.'s sent taxicabs.
On Sunday the officers came themselves
in motor-cars.   She could not bear peace.

When I was a small boy, too,
I admired Hitler.
More than anyone else,
I think.   Looking in the fire
imagining descent of fire
upon the bunker.   Think
of it, to bring down your world
in marvellous ruins around you.
I would like to do as much.

Surely there was no more violence
in Hitler than in Van Gogh.
That other painter, that other fire.

"On the Beach": A Nuclear Disarmament Showing

Some have been tormented by the truth of all.
There is certainly about this reckless woman
Something of the lost but always remembered Eden
To which all turning tends.
We observe her with suspended disbelief:
The contours of a face etched in candle-shadow
Are bones dreaming out the rain and windy dark
Of a time redeemed by its own ending.

The point is there must be catastrophe
If there is going to be this unreeling dream,
The healing slow-motion of happiness.
The halcyon floats out the winter solstice
Fourteen days from Thanatos.
Therefore, if you would love perfectly and wholly,
Be advised
That you must look to the boots battering the stair
Climbing the attic of Rotterdam
And to the furies converging on Hiroshima.

In the ruins of Pompeii was found
A curious and touching tableau of petrified lovers.
If you only knew, I thought, about the iceberg ahead of
    time,
Or about the blood
Rhythmic and merry in the streets of Johannesburg.
Or if you knew
You were to be incinerated
Shortly in a fire-storm over Dresden.

Old Poet to the Young

I was not glib as you,
birdtongued youth.   I had a stammer.
And I was innocent far longer,
strong in artifice because estranged from life.

Now I have three daughters, and a charming wife,
and a considerable gift for public speech.
I am involved far more than you can be
with real life.   I have the assurance
of policies –
a mortgaged house, an island, an XKE
(my one extravagance)
and a Chair of Poetry.   Moreover,
my quiet heart is untrustworthy,
the doctor confirms the vision of my left eye
has seriously deteriorated, and I begin
secretly to be doubtful of my old age.

The wind, this season's blustering,
is my increasing dread.   Remember
I have seen and known and done
murder
and looted with the best of warriors.   More,
I have burned my eyes behind a secret door
and I have found no Colonus.

You are different.   Leaves
to you are spring dancers
perpetually renewed.   Phoenixes
leap out of your pitiless, impatient eye.
Until I cannot talk to you,
I cannot tell you.

You come as gusty as the equinox,
whole zodiacs of sadness quite contained
you are so light, or else
so deep in dream.   I see this.   The pain,
the flame that burns the vision clean
and cold as the destroying moon
is in your grin, your goblin step.

O jaunty spring heart, troubled happily,
what is your secret?
That you turn forever on the fevered hill –
your face bright as wind, white
like lightning
to all the ending of my unremembered hopes.

A Parting Word for the Young Lyric Poet

Mole.   Mole's his nature
who burrows in earth.
Gnome too.   Watch
for sly, gnomic evasions.

Troll.   Hear him speak
ex cathedra –
anguished troll hoarding
his ridiculous pride.

He opens
the door, hesitant
upon the morning,
peers at the needling light

then slams it fast,
hops to perform
his panicky exorcism.
A well-turned quatrain or two.

Mole.   Does he think
his bungled
agonies matter?
So much elegiac glitter

impairs vision, blocks
truth, parodies pain
that lives in living
fire even in earth.

Words in Exile

Notes from a London Diary

I

Specimen Scholar

Morning
on Southampton Row.   I gasp
like a fish
drowning in air.   A pale

disc of flame
tints the day
poisonous yellow.

Crushed
in the coloured slide
I flounder

to the fetid
B.M.

crouch behind
sooted walls like
one of the antiquities.

II

Nov. 23, 1966

To be left
alone where
there is no vision.

Drunk, strange, alone.

24

How pathetically
I reach
for the one person
I have met
that I seem to belong to.

III

Nov. 29, 1966

The strange
daytime twilight –

This grey twilight
at three o'clock –

I come home
drunk.

This thing
floods the room
with a mysterious radiance.

I cannot bear
to turn on the lights.

IV

London Nocturne

My nerves are shot.
The sky is bruised blue.
A moon like a torn nail.
Hundreds of city things float
across my sight.
Hundreds of insects.
I hate them all
indiscriminately.

Man Walking

There is a man
walking.   Against brown
uneven stone
caught in the sun.
He wears a car-coat
and stovepipe trousers.

He sees himself
in series in
the eyelike dark
uneven windows of
passing cars: a long
disjointed man

who walks
toward the square
against brown
uneven stone.
The chances are
he will never get there.

Zurich: April, 1967

I

Snow-clouds
have blurred
the mountain edges.
Last evening's
snows are gone.

II

I dream of
terrifying
sunlit and empty
landscapes where
I cannot find you.

Go Then

Go then. Be free, infrequent
As the flowerings of snow;
Those interlocking stars, fixed
In movement, go

As you must go. As music,
Motionless. As water moves
A finely patterned stillness:
Meshes, creases, grooves.

As white and wandering moon, move
At your unity
And keep (old paradox)
That frozen constancy,

Revoke your snow in tides,
Resume the charted sky,
Take and reject and take with an
Austere and distant eye.

and Penelope

I am writing this
for you, Margrit
(and Penelope, for you).

Do you remember
the snails, Margrit, red
by the castle at Fredensborg
moving infinitely slow
and moist in the forest
on the damp ground under
sun-drenched foliage?

It is strange what I remember.

That we walked
to the dimpled lake but not
of what we spoke.   Only
paths, incredibly tall trees
(their shaken lights after rain)
on the castle-grounds at Fredensborg.

And that I thought you
womanly, being there
in your apartment partaking
in cool lightnings of late June.
That I thought you
sensible and kind – even wise
after the way of women.

And how I teased you about
the burning of witches
the Danish male's only revenge
watching yellow tongues lick a way
into the cold blue Scandinavian dusk
the cloud shapes running at the east
sitting on a sea-wall at Elsinore.

And your cool merry laughter
as a child laughs, only there was
expense of nervous tension.

(Lovers, at midnight, move apart
at snail's pace)

Margrit, I am writing it for you
(a poem, a low flame)
for your expectation and
your childlike gaiety

for the humour
and the sadness in me
that would turn you into "literature".

Niagara II

Late light separates blades
of grass.

Now the train
slithers into the vinelands.   Home.
Whose grapes ripen
slowly.

Field after field
of vines.

The place rich, burnished
with summer.

The poet sardonic,
awkward.

Canadians are so
unfinished.

The End of an Incident

There were two boys swimming.

One stands and looks
on a wall of stained glass.
It resembles a surface of water
in a cold, north lake.
The other shouts in panic

as he comes up for air.
There's a corpse down there.
Christ, bleeding, redlit
metal Christ on the wall.
He floats on the blue glass.

He is intensely white.
They say it is suicide.
They put a blanket over him.
Later, in the hot sun, a small
trickle, dark, comes from underneath.

I came out of the ruined church.

Wedding in Canada

A blind savagery of snow rages.
Blizzard, ripped veil in the screaming air,
invents a church, perilous, white.
The sleeping river is invisible.

Yet cruel incandescence of ice shifts
and vibrates.   Girl confused, boy lost
and drowning in an underworld of his own make
are lately, doubtfully, met.

Their pasts – blind, possible hurt – must mate.
Their lusts – sick, turbulent – breed
a visionary spring, purer being.
The tree creaks in the seething yard.

But the low stove crackles its indifferent tongues.
The sleeping river flows invisible.
Till hands reach, touching, and the breath
invents a church, perilous, white.

Chalice Well and Glastonbury Tor

I

"In the sacred
garden of the
Chalice Well
a great sleep

fell on my mind,
and I saw only
the enormous roses
huge with colour."

II

Standing on
Glastonbury Tor
amid Arthurian, placid,
dung-spattered cows,

I saw the high holy
particularity of men,
threshers, hedge, radiant
green fields.

Eastwood: April, 1967

On the tall brick
street where D. H.
Lawrence was born
a boy in turtle-
neck, faded jeans

revs his motor-
bike, doesn't look
the long way down
that looks toward
open country.

Pop Song for New Year's: 1968

Birds crack the cold shell of sky.
The white sun slouches through bare trees
too empty of green to be dejected.
The dogs frisk, their turds are holy.
Richard goes up to Arabella, bombs fall,
Lorenzo burns but not for Hilda.

Ménage à trois in Mecklenburgh Square.
Virginia Woolf's house was bombed
in the second war, her mind broken
like the moon caught in corrugated ice.
That other, five years ago, stumbled
into The Lamb, frantic in a turban.

Baroque pain, structured pain.
What good was their love, their genius?
The trees are spiders on the blank day.
The Regency fronts keep white through
year after year.   Vomit splatters
on the pavement like an action painting.

Baroque pain, structured pain.
Bid me to live, and I will live, sang Hilda.
Lorenzo burns, bombs fall through air
too empty of God to be rejected.
Birds crack the cold shell of sky.
The dogs frisk, their turds are holy.

Words in Exile

I

As the year
moves to its darkness, I move
walk, run, cross Russell Square
in the fugitive sunlight.   Pigeons,
leaves are flying.   Red hydrangeas
burn on the air.   Glowing
coals of solstice.   How your cheeks grew
hollow with dark
two years ago.

II

LONDON,
the great Beast.   Paper
crackles in the flames, no sky, only white
Presence in the air.   I walk
run, cross Russell Square
in the fugitive sunlight.
Think: Agincourt, the burgeoning earth inhabited
by many dead.

III

When my grand-
mother, ELLEN, was buried, not there
but at Niagara, the wind twisted the earth, stung
on the false face of grief.   Leaves
rattled along the earth.

IV

The trees
in England are ghostly, behind the eyes
surpassing the moon.   Whose white limbs
are theirs, her comeliness.   Whose limbs
are white in a thin
drizzle of rain.   Trees
are beautiful, and not dismayed
at mere human grief.   They turn
on the air.   They dance.

V

MATTHEW, my grand-
father died at 93.   He did not dance.   And if
he burned it was the cold burning of snow.   He did not
    know
how to dance.   And fire fell on him.   His bones
burn in the burgeoning earth of Agincourt.

VI

And I
shivered that day, in sunlight, fugitive, I
whirling, a leaf caught, and carried to darkness, space,
    falling
outward from earth, from air, a black
desolate astronaut.

VII

Paper
crackles in the flames, no sky, only white
Presence in the air.   Still the rain
holds off, and the humid square
smells like a lover's body.   You
are living still.   As the year.

VIII

Trees
are beautiful, and not dismayed.   Pigeons,
leaves are flying.   Red hydrangeas
burn on the air.   I move
walk, run.   In the white
Presence of the air.   The humid square
smells like a lover's body.   You
are living still
like a solstice coal.

These Islands

Two Kinds of Islands

Turning morning, turning to mirrors
I do not find you now.
Not dream of islands, not
Follow the longing eye, I said
To you, morning sky unread.

To you, morning sky unread,
Follow the longing eye, I said.
Not dream of islands, not
I do not find you now
Turning morning, turning to mirrors.

I pretend, too

The wooden owl pretends
he doesn't know me.
Sits on a log and looks
across park.   It is my birthday.

A park is round.   A lake
has many gaping planes.
I am 28.   Trees
rebuke with tall silence.

Useless trade.   Hunter
trapped in wood.   Kids
play hockey in the street.
Their sticks are wood.

I am 28.   There is
a wooden owl above my balcony.
He pretends he doesn't know.
And me, I pretend, too.

now trees expand

now trees expand like suns –
the park after rain
holds measureless spaces of light
though there is no sun
but only dark verticals and places
of green translucence –
and I feel somehow
transparent, the walls
of the apartment dissolve
till it is all window, all transparent

and there is no sun
but the blue roots
coil darkly, coil and flash
like stylized lightning –
now trees expand like suns
shaking galaxies of green
though there is no sun –

when there is sun
each conflagration of leaf
feeds on the green air
now there is only grey
transparency and absence
there is no sun
there is only silence
filling these spaces
where trees expand like suns

Interior Monologue # 666

"Hydrocephalics are holy, too,
they have
a certain
bloated beatitude . . ."

I think I am becoming
a tree.   At any rate
something slow, lethargic,
vegetable.   I am said
to resemble a rutabaga.

Do rutabagas have leaves
I wonder?   I should like
to have leaves at least.
Slow ones.   Leaves of pain
perhaps.   Leaves of sleep.

It is said the gods
descend at last.   In U.F.O.'s
perhaps.   In B.V.D.'s for all
I care.   Who cares if gods
descend?   They are leaves

of sky, my leaves.   Mine,
perhaps yours, I would be generous.
Every day the sky has leaves.
The sky-tree has grey leaves.
The sky-tree is ours.

Riding in Colin's Boat (the poetics thereof

Drunk, we slop and throb
on water.   The boat
bends and sways about
crazily.   The shoreline leans,
burns.

On the sky bobs
Christ the Astronaut.

(we poets fink out
of our unbearable visions
observe now the birds
of purgatory settle
dull brown sea
faces blank again

CHRIST THE ASTRONAUT
BURNS ON THE SKY
NAKED WITH LUST AND PAIN

Hold to it.   Hold
to Christ the Astronaut.

(now the place is reached

A reddish wake of sun
touches the drunken lake.
The motor cuts.   The boat's
thrust and lurch give way.

The island of birds arises.

"Near Kingston
country heat
is hotter
than city heat."

In country heat –
Yarker, East Camden –
the blowtorch air beats
on the red Triumph.

Sitting by Fred (fanatic,
bent on auctions) my mind
bends from the crackling
road to the glazed river.

In country heat –
tar roads, snake fences –
Fred looks for auctions.
His countryside reels with visions

of washstands, Boston rockers;
my mind is dizzy anti-matter.
Doughbox and ladderback fade,
facts and fingertips.

The riverbed lurches right.
The blowtorch air beats
on the red Triumph.
The parched grass yellows.

Nightfall.   The kamikaze swallows
dip out of city sight.
Fred works over his rocker
under a naked bulb

in his garage.   My mind
glazes and crackles.   I
glare out of my high window where
facts and fingertips fuse.

In country heat –
Battersea, Picton –
the blowtorch air beats
on the red Triumph.

Sequiturs

"[Life is a] partial self-realization of the
potentialities of atomic electron states."
     – *J. D. Bernal*, The Origin of Life

The persistence of the dead in the living,
if recognized, makes us sane.
This park is a wood where brown
men walked. As I walk. Now.
The squirrels eruptions of earth.
Myself an explosion of whirling dust.

(Twisted gum-trees stand in the bush
near Brisbane. Dark, still
Aborigines on the high ridge. At Delphi,
too, the afternoon sun broke into fields of flowers.
But then, even squirrels persist. And not just
in memory. The cells of the brain disintegrate.)

Atomize the wood. The brave, the vast
animal that lives alone, deathless
as dust. Man, plant, bird alive –
all things are alive, then. Dust
is a winged life before and after life,
immortal bird made of cosmic fire.

We have not known our demons, truly.
Even cars, boats, are alive.
The persistence of the dead in the living,
if recognized, makes us sane.
Must we live again the brave's painful death
in our machine-cities, these grotesque disguises?

48

The Art of Loving

We have no choice, really, about love.
We are composites, all of us.
From Peter Sellers talking to himself
to Catherine declaring, "I *am* Heathcliff!"

Or think of Orpheus, if you've a mind,
descending into his own dark.
Breaking shadows.
To exalt a fragment
is false, however.   Look too hard
and you will lose what you cannot articulate.

Always we are seeking Persephone.   But she
becomes enamoured of her dusky Dis.
Always is a corridor of mirrors,
the turning of Lot's wife.

Be still, then.   Pray
for all your failed loves.   Pray
for courage with purpose,
for stillness with concern.

Others may wonder about God.   I do not care.
We are all God, if we are anything.
This is to say
nothing, of course.   Nonetheless

I have said
everything.   That is why
it does not matter if you heard me or not.

Poem on Good Friday

I

The wind today is mind's apocalypse.
The fine park disintegrates in sound
that floods the landscape with anxiety.
The wheeling of those strident gulls
arouses and allays the questioning
in which the heart interrogates the heart.
The question is a kind of answering.

II

"What is there then to do when I know
already that longing is insatiable,
that not any love, no, not any fulfilment
is ever enough for the whoring heart?"

And I was April-brained, once, too,
am still young enough to imagine
the lineaments of Eden in the raucous call
of April gulls hawking their crude crucifixion
over the whole earth.

III

There is no end to their crying,
no peace in the scattered sky
of their accomplished dissonance, their chaos
bent to the creaking trees.   Subtle
as premonitions our lives move
into the waves' intense and shifting frequencies.

Can the mind burning
in the wind's design
then seize?   Die
to the earth's taut
and hungry turning?

Gulls scream.
The gnarled words break.

IV

The mind sets.   But the heart,
luckily intractable, rebelliously will not give up.
The mind learns treachery will be the thing,
the value and virtue of fragility.   Finally
only tension is creative.   Gull-cries
echo in the marriage-bed.   All quest,
all questioning affirms, announces
the answer to desire is desire.

Astrology

It's an approach.   Say what you like
about it.   It's an approach.
Speak of the transience of philosophies;
all are de-commissioned at last.
I admit this.   It's entirely the point.

I care more about this
arrangement of words than about you.
To return one needs an approach,
"a way of happening",
and any approach will do
in a sense.   The one that works
is true (of course, all are true).

Why not then take the intricate
fire of stars as way?   Interlocking roses
of our summer day
are no less blasted in the tides of dust.
Why not take penmanship, ornithology?
Why not take you and me?

Can you give me of your
bare instincts enough?   Save me
(though the cost may be beyond your ken)?
Do it then.   For I know.   But
I must know the full horoscope
of your desire.   So give me
conjunctions of dust; make again
the knotted turning of the seasons start;
give me the whole fire of your heart.

Alchemy

Agnes Sorel was the mistress of that king
whom Joan of Arc also served

Agnes Sorel et Jeanne d'Arc
Wrestled beauty from the dark.
Who will say which rose could bring
Greater pleasure to the King?

Opening the rose of dream,
Seeding fire in the stream,
Other practised magic spells.
One heard voices in the bells.

Honi soit qui mal y pense.
Better to break into dance
Than to ponder womanhood,
Maidenhead or greater good.

Greater pleasure to the King
Who will say which one could bring?
Other voices in the blood,
One heard voices in the wood.

Maidenhead or greater good.
Better to break into dance
Like the windy leaf of chance
In the bleak ancestral wood.

In the bleak ancestral wood
Like the windy leaf of chance
Better to break into dance,
Maidenhead or greater good.

One heard voices in the wood,
Other voices in the blood.
Who will say which one could bring
Greater pleasure to the King?

Maidenhead or greater good.
Than to ponder womanhood
Better to break into dance.
Honi soit qui mal y pense.

One heard voices in the bells,
Other practised magic spells,
Seeding fire in the stream,
Opening the rose of dream.

Greater pleasure to the King
Who will say which rose could bring?
Wrestled beauty from the dark
Agnes Sorel et Jeanne d'Arc.

Spaces

I would love you as I do the land
so be
stillness of lake in the broken forest,
black lilt and ripple
of lake darkening with the day
(for here
our only clearings are water),

or be
a green space choked with birds
and darknesses that live in light
and leaf
alone as pain or paradise
their little dreams and deaths,

for water is a black
silence in our hearts,
and green
is memory of what never was
except eternally,

and we are one
with blackness of rain
realized
over the crested islands of our peace,

and look
look, the children are running
there on the floor of the forest
in a green light running,
taking their gleaming
sunlight spaces
away into the dark lake forever.

55

Speedboat

The machine, many poets
to the contrary, is not
the enemy.

In our just becoming
world, we wish
on motors as on stars.
All the same.   All the best
hopes are for motion.

Spray. Wind. Space.
Reclaimed, a way home.
Disintegrating in gladness,
stung into sweetest pain,
we are racing.

We are racing
to the lost islands
of apples and birds,
islands of wild apples
breaking in flame
behind the eye,

islands of trees
where the nested gulls
alarmed, rise to cry, o cry
the heart's wisdom down
in whirling explosions
that meet and dwindle
our brokenwinged myth.

For everything we do
is the attempt, blind,
speedblown, to unlock
that fire, that fevering
atom's flight that makes
forever back
the winged trajectory,
the strenuous and timeless track.

Derangement

Islands are green mandalas
that turn upon their light.
Bright nerve-tips of wave
curve into air like the faces
of Rilke's rapt angels.

Out in the bays that heave
the afternoon moon's phases
sailboats are elliptical triangles.
Angles of innocent air make delight
of troubled swallows' carving.

Very slowly now we are leaving
our senses in hallowed night.
Sight burns us free of love
to green paraphrase
that burns us finally free of sight.

Macdonald Park

The structure of "Macdonald Park" perhaps requires some comment. The poem is meant to be spoken by two voices that sometimes blend into a single voice. In Part I a vision of Sir John Macdonald, the first Prime Minister and chief architect of the Canadian Confederation, emerges from a park in Kingston, Ontario. In Part II the speaker of the poem addresses Sir John, suggesting that there are parallels between his experience and that of such "explorers" as Sam Slick, Susanna Moodie, Archibald Lampman, Josh Smith, and others. Part III deals with Macdonald's life, incorporating remarks he made at various times, and Part IV with the coming of spring to the park. The poem follows the curve of the seasons from late fall to early spring. Overlooking the park, which changes its shape with the seasons, I came to feel there was a thing in it, a vision or Beast, to be observed and recorded. The reader may decide who he was and whether he got away.

I

(the yellow tree
that stands
in my window
delicate, imperial

moves to some end
I cannot see
some paradox
some lie

that I begin
to formulate
here

                    Sir John may know.
                    It's his park.
                    All this scattered
                    gold is his.

                    Perhaps
                    under the great
                    roots that coil
                    he lies

                    a giant
                    or a gnome.

                    A red-nosed gnome.
                    Lord of Misrule.
                    Alberich
                    scattered under gold.

                    Given to earth, earthy.
                    Thus alive.

Capricorn.
The prancing goat.
Bibulous, sly.
Kingston's Pan.

The picnicking god
among his people.

(later
  the plucked
  tree
  naked

The eyes are glazed, fixed
on some unseen skyline.
The mouth bestows blessings.

He does not bore them
with facts. Dances
among the cakes. Dances.

The whiskey-throated folk
murmuring; their proud horses
tied outside the grove.

On the crisp air
images of coming
apple-thud.

(sunlight
perpendicular
on
limestone

promises
the snow

(perhaps
a lie
may be
true north

Years later,
climbing the snow-hill, he looked back
a moment – trees striped with white
shadows, negative. The waste lake
between and beyond. And he said
then, something might be made
of this wood. Nodded to himself
and went on.

falling in the park outside my window the flakes
are falling falling soundless on the beaten earth Sir John
Alexander Macdonald stands a titan in a circle of light
night and the boundless snowlight falling falling a white
fire a suffused lightning the silence of the opening
sky the fevering solstice flower the heaven streaming
sea

images gather in the gathering dark dark
amid the blaze of snow light the light blazing into
the head white shadows forming in the formless dark
the dark insubstantial as foam Sir John is dancing
behind the window dancing among the flakes dancing
behind chaos behind within the rent seething air the
window

II

The explorers, those who walk
in a waste place
unceasingly.
These we celebrate.

The squire, a cultivated
Sancho Panza, itinerant in judgement.
Sam Slick, his alter ego
(we also are Americans)
pushing clocks on the timeless.
Mrs. Moodie, her absurd
gentility giving meaning
to the meaningless trees'
black tangle on the white sky.

(Roberts, moving yet on the high
green hill over Tantramar, needed
the distance from which he looks.
Carman, his cousin, not so lucky

as to have found distance,
made of our vagueness
a virtue, a voice for loss
and the uncertain floods of longing.)

Lampman, like Quixote, strove
against a windmill's whine and whirr.
You mightn't have known that.
He had it in for your pet Leviathan.

His friend, Scott, that promising boy
you hired when he was 17 –
he quarried a hill of gold
changing it gradually to steel.

These are called
"ancestral voices". And some
of them are much like you.

Take that handyman, Josh Smith,
patching up his leaking ark
bound for – where?

                    Turbulent days,
apparently. Icebergs. Cold baptismals
under sea

(where a poet meets the silent
leviathan   and another
is drowning under closed
waters

         a third   alone
     and on the shifting
     edge   cries out

     another hibernates   & one
     with a clown's defiant frenzy
     swims and sings
     gladly to the white   sudden

     sun)

Anyhow, snow falls.
Grey, relentless.
Winter fevers into winter dreams.

This a winter land
no spring has entered.

III

"I had no boyhood",
you said once.
Yet all your life
was wintry boyhood.

A strange light
danced in the snow you touched.

Once, in the States
you turned
to cracked concertina, larked
with dancing

bears, danced too
for coin, danced
reckless
blue eyes flickering like snow.

Could you see
then   (as I see)
islands, a tarnished
lake that turned
and turns, endlessly
serene in tension

                    (and
                      endlessly park
                      give trees
                      up to hard
                      starlight, till

                    trees
                    are tuning forks)?

Though winter has lyric moods
the blizzard raged in your blood;
behind the windows   flashed
intimations of landscape.

And now, Isabella is dying.
Slowly. You cannot help her.
Her eyes burn down. Slowly
they lose focus. Lose

all hope of landscape.

You turn to the window
's vacant space, turn
outward to inward   grace

> "We have desired in this
> measure
> to declare
>
> in the most
> solemn and emphatic
> manner
>
> our resolve
> to be under
> the Sovereignty
>
> of Your Majesty
> and your family
> for ever."

you walked upon the lake
sometimes
sunlight
turned surfaces bright

on the snow
your shadow was duskblue

> You were drunk at Russell's hotel,
> at Lévis, in Halifax. You kept
> Her Majesty's man waiting. You
> were holed-up with port, and you
> danced your slow shadows to the blue
> dark turning measures of snow.

67

Your dancing has changed us.

You danced a dance of steel
and we are changed.
These odysseys that bind
the heart to distances
have changed us.

You danced a dance of rope, too.

"He shall hang, though
every dog in Quebec
bark in his favour."

on the snow
your shadow was duskblue

Imperial arrogance? Jingoist
for votes or in earnest?
I suspect a boy's mirth behind
your last cries of treason.

You died still British, still P.M.,
still a boy. You had gained
a last midwinter time.
The blue trees of evening

turned
upon your time.

you walked upon the lake
sometimes
sunlight

turned surfaces bright

> Near the end
> Laurier came. Matters
> of adjournment. Light
> breaking in the deep wood
>
> streaking it gold.
>
> "Nice chap that. If I
> were twenty years younger he'd
> be my colleague . . ."
>
> Mutterings
> in the inner room: "Old,
> too old . . ."

on the snow
your shadow is duskblue

IV

the grey crying of gulls announces
rain

> the grey crying of gulls
> on the grey sky
> the bending of wet boughs   the
>
> slow fuse of sun
> > suspended

Comes then
the ambiguous spring.

"I was
exhilarated, yet
not sure
that I could bear
those icy gold springs."

slow fuse of sun
                    suspended

          Sir John may know.
          It's his park.

(the gold
 buds
 waken
 in light

 though lean
 trees
 keep
 their dark

Coda

the park is eternal but I
fall beyond it in the fabulous
whole and silent angel of fire
flying the wound that sings

looking out my window I see
park and lake, leaf and lost desire
curved as music or the universe
to the old eye, the androgynous wings

that move, and moving make
an end of echoes, a virtue
of shifting perspectives, a thing
finally complete, and whole, and moving

Envoi

How shall I list my failures?

For a beginning the red
bright sumacs at Bevan Heights, so red
they make the leaves green fire. Smoke
was blue on the hills, the orchards. And the mud-
brown fire of the Arno, the black bridges. At the stroke
of twelve thick blue snow was falling
over London. Sand-coloured
leaves are falling, heaving at the hot ground.
Dusk, a deep white and whitening
dusk on chalk-walls at Mykonos. I remember
hitching, boys on a crowded bus
near Aberdeen, warm blasphemies
holding off the mist. I remember
the snakelike
thrashing of crowd and motorcade, the slow
explosion of rose. I remember
a cat tensed in dusk. Lemon
leaves glow in the Sicilian mornings.
I remember. This and this and this.
The metallic
aquamarine inlets. The moon
on the turning sky.

The islands of your lost body.